1

IN THE WITCH'S KITCHEN
Poems for Halloween

IN THE WITCH'S KITCHEN

Poems for Halloween

Compiled by John E. Brewton,

Lorraine A. Blackburn,

George M. Blackburn III

ILLUSTRATED BY Harriett Barton

Thomas Y. Crowell   New York

Text copyright © 1980 by John E. Brewton,
Lorraine A. Blackburn, and George M. Blackburn
Illustrations copyright © 1980 by Harriett Barton
All rights reserved. Printed in the United States of America.
No part of this book may be used or reproduced in any manner
whatsoever without written permission except in the case of
brief quotations embodied in critical articles and reviews.
For information address Thomas Y. Crowell, 10 East 53rd Street,
New York, N.Y. 10022. Published simultaneously in Canada by
Fitzhenry & Whiteside Limited, Toronto.

Library of Congress Cataloging in Publication Data
Main entry under title:
In the witch's kitchen.
Includes indexes.
1. Halloween—Juvenile poetry. 2. Children's
poetry, American. I. Brewton, John Edmund, 1898–
II. Blackburn, Lorraine A. III. Blackburn, G.
Meredith. IV. Barton, Harriett.
PS595.H3515 1980   811'.008'033   79-7822
ISBN 0-690-04061-X   ISBN 0-690-04062-8 (lib. bdg.)

1 2 3 4 5 6 7 8 9 10
First Edition

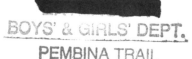

ACKNOWLEDGMENTS

Grateful acknowledgment is made to the following publishers, authors, and other copy-right holders.

Abingdon Press for "Halloween" by Ivy O. Eastwick from *I Rode the Black Horse Far Away* by Ivy O. Eastwick, copyright © 1960 by Abingdon Press. Used by permission.

Atheneum Publishers, Inc., for "The Skeleton Walks" and "Wicked Witch's Kitchen" by X. J. Kennedy from *One Winter Night in August and Other Nonsense Jingles* by X. J. Kennedy (A Margaret K. McElderry Book), copyright © 1975 by X. J. Kennedy; and "Whose Boo Is Whose?" by X. J. Kennedy from *The Phantom Ice Cream Man: More Nonsense Verse* by X. J. Kennedy (A Margaret K. McElderry Book), copyright © 1979 by X. J. Kennedy; "Haiku for Halloween" by Myra Cohn Livingston from *4-Way Stop and Other Poems* by Myra Cohn Livingston (A Margaret K. McElderry Book), copyright © 1976 by Myra Cohn Livingston; "Do Ghouls?," "I'm Skeleton," "No TV," and "We Three" by Lilian Moore from *See My Lovely Poison Ivy* by Lilian Moore, copyright © 1975 by Lilian Moore. Used by permission of Atheneum Publishers.

Child Life Magazine for "The Mini Spooks" by Eloise Anderson from *Child Life* Maga-zine, copyright © 1970 by Review Publishing Co., Inc., Indianapolis, Indiana. Reprinted by permission of the publisher.

William Cole for "Beware, My Child" by Shel Silverstein from *Oh, What Nonsense* by William Cole, published by Viking Press, Inc. Poem copyright © 1966 by Shel Silverstein; and "On Halloween" by Shel Silverstein from *Poems for Seasons and Celebrations* edited by William Cole, published by World Publishing Co. Poem copyright © 1961 by Shel Silverstein.

Doubleday & Company, Inc., for "The Bat" by Theodore Roethke from *The Collected Poems of Theodore Roethke*, copyright © 1938 by Theodore Roethke. Reprinted by permission of Doubleday & Company, Inc.

Farrar, Straus & Giroux, Inc., for "Haunted House" and "Pumpkin," reprinted by per-mission of Farrar, Straus & Giroux, Inc., from *More Small Poems* by Valerie Worth. Copyright © 1976 by Valerie Worth.

Aileen Fisher for her poem "Witch in the Wintry Wood" from *Ghosts and Goblins* by Wilhelmina Harper, published by E. P. Dutton & Co., Inc., copyright © 1936, '64, '65. Reprinted by permission of the author.

I like winter, spring, summer, and fall.
In the fall I like fall best of all.
　　What I like most is
　　A witch or a ghost is
Quite likely to pay me a call.

—*Beatrice Schenk de Regnier*

"It's cold," said the cricket,
"my fingers are numb.
I scarcely can fiddle,
I scarcely can strum.
And, oh, I'm so sleepy,
now summer has gone."
He dropped his fiddle
to stifle a yawn.

"Don't," said the field mouse, "act so sober.
You can't stop yet, when it's still October."

"I've played," said the cricket,
"for weeks and weeks.
My fiddle needs fixing,
it's full of squeaks.
My fingers need resting."
He yawned. "Ho, hum . . .
I'm quite (yawn) ready . . .
for winter to come.

I've found me the coziest . . .
        doziest . . .
        house . . ."

"You can't stop *now*," said his friend, the mouse.

"No?" yawned the cricket,
and closed his eyes.
"I've played so much
for a chap my size,
it's time (he yawned)
for my winter snooze:
I hear the creak
of November's shoes."

"You can't," said the mouse in a voice of sorrow,
"you can't stop fiddling until tomorrow.
Tune up your fiddle for one last scene . . .
have you forgotten it's Halloween?"

"What!" cried the cricket.
He yawned no more!
"You should have mentioned
the fact before.
Is everyone ready?
And where's the score?
What in the world
are we waiting for?"
The cricket fiddled,
the field mouse squeaked,
the dry weeds twiddled,
the bare twigs tweaked,

the hoot owl hooted,
the cornstalks strummed,
the west wind tooted,
the fence wires hummed:

Oh, what a concert, all night long!
The fiddle was shrill, and the wind was strong:
    "Halloween, Halloween,
            crick,
            crack,
            creak.
    Halloween, Halloween,
            scritch,
            scratch,
            squeak."

—*Aileen Fisher*

If the moon shines
On the black pines
And an owl flies
And a ghost cries
And the hairs rise
On the back
 on the back
  on the back of your neck—

If you look quick
At the moon-slick
On the black air
And what goes there
Rides a broom-stick
And if things pick
At the back
 at the back
  at the back of your neck—

Would you know then
By the small men
With the lit grins
And with no chins,
By the owl's hoo,
And the ghost's boo,
By the Tom Cat,
And the Black Bat
On the night air,
And the thing there,
By the thing,
      by the thing,
           by the dark thing there

(Yes, you do,
      yes, you do
           know the thing I mean)

That it's now,
  that it's now,
    that it's—Halloween!

—John Ciardi

Goblins on the doorstep,
  Phantoms in the air,
Owls on witches' gateposts
  Giving stare for stare,
Cats on flying broomsticks,
  Bats against the moon,
Stirrings round of fate-cakes
  With a solemn spoon,
Whirling apple parings,
  Figures draped in sheets
Dodging, disappearing,
  Up and down the streets,
Jack-o'-lanterns grinning,
  Shadows on a screen,
Shrieks and starts and laughter—
  This is Halloween!

—*Dorothy Brown Thompson*

Witches flying past on broomsticks,
 Black cats leaping here and there,
White-robed spooks on every corner,
 Mournful moaning in the air,

Goblins peering out of windows,
 Spirit-things that rap and run—
But don't be scared—it's just October,
 Having one last hour of fun!

—*Mary Jane Carr*

On Halloween I'll go to town
And wear my trousers upside down,
And wear my shoes turned inside out
And wear a wig of sauerkraut.

—Shel Silverstein

Halloween,
Halloween,
Halloween!

Latch the latch,
Catch the catch,
Scratch the match.

Witches ride,
Jack will hide
Lantern-eyed.

Better bake.
Better make
Candy, cake.

Mask or sheet:
Trick or treat!
Ghosts are fleet.

Soon or late
Sure as fate
Goes the gate.

Knocker, bell
Cast the spell.
Treat them well!

Silly sooth:
Youth is youth
Tongue and tooth.

Treat them quick,
Else the trick:
Take your pick!

—David McCord

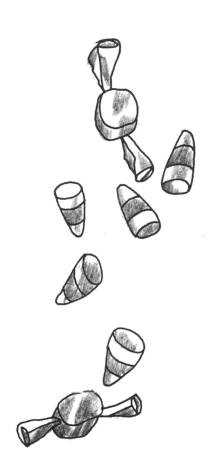

We three
went out on Halloween.
A Pirate
An Ape
A Witch between.

We went from door to door.

By the light
of the moon
these shadows were seen
A Pirate
An Ape
A Witch between
and—

Say, how did we get to be FOUR?

—Lilian Moore

It's the time of year
For goblins . . . big and small.
Watch out for the mini spooks!
They're the peskiest ones of all.

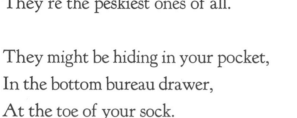

They might be hiding in your pocket,
In the bottom bureau drawer,
At the toe of your sock.
Almost any place they think
They're not likely to be caught.

They go about their mischief
Making not a sound.
Still, you'll know they've been there
By the tricks on those around.

They pull buttons off your coat,
Make the hinges creak,
Take your hankies,

Pinch your toes,
Cause ice cream cones to leak.

They rattle windows, mess your hair,
Stretch rubber bands till they snap.
Tip the milk, steal puzzle pieces . . .
And they don't stop with that.

Sometimes they're downright naughty,
In many mini ways.
They untie shoes, slam the door,
And hide the jacket that you know
You hung in place the night before.

Some stay around all year, they say,
But Halloween's their night to play.
Take care! Beware
Of those wee little mini spooks
Pulling on your costume,

Tearing the bottom of your sack,
Blowing out your jack-o'-lantern
From somewhere behind your back.

Don't be afraid . . .
Take a deep breath . . .
Turn around. Face them.
That's the thing to do.
But all the while,
Be expecting a tiny little "Boo!"

—*Eloise Anderson*

Whatever is inside that sheet
Just gave a dreadful shout!

A-ha, but what about those feet
That I see sticking out?

They help me guess who's hiding there,
Whose eyes are peeking through:

And how could anyone be scared
Of You!

—*Dorothy Aldis*

Monsters do *not* scare me much,

Nor do goblins and ghosts and all such.

   But on Halloween night

   Please hold my hand tight—

I don't want to be out of touch.

—*Beatrice Schenk de Regnier*

When the moon
rides high,
up overhead—
and I am snug
and warm,
in bed—
in the autumn dark
the ghosts move 'round,
making their
mournful,
moaning sound.

I listen to know
when the ghosts
go by.
I hear a wail,
and I hear
a sigh.

But I can't quite tell
which I hear
the most—
the wind,
or the wail
or some passing ghost.

—*Author Unknown*

Two ghosts I know once traded heads
And shrieked and shook their sheets to shreds—
"You're me!" yelled one, "and me, I'm you!
Now who can boo the loudest boo?"

"Me!" cried the other, and for proof
He booed a boo that scared the roof
Right off our house. The TV set
Jumped higher than a jumbo jet.

The first ghost snickered. "Why, you creep,
Call that a boo? That feeble beep?
Hear *this*!"—and sucking in a blast
Of wind, he puffed his sheet so vast

And booed so hard, a passing goose
Lost all its down. The moon shook loose
And fell and smashed to smithereens—
Stars scattered like spilled jellybeans.

"How's that for booing, boy? I win,"
Said one. The other scratched a chin
Where only bone was—"Win or lose?
How can we tell whose boo is whose?"

—X. J. Kennedy

There was an old wife and she lived all alone
    In a cottage not far from Hitchin:
And one bright night, by the full moon light,
    Comes a ghost right into her kitchen.

About that kitchen neat and clean
    The ghost goes pottering round.
But the poor old wife is deaf as a boot
    And so hears never a sound.

The ghost blows up the kitchen fire,
    As bold as bold can be;
He helps himself from the larder shelf,
    But never a sound hears she.

He blows on his hands to make them warm,
    And whistles aloud, "Whee-hee!"
But still as a sack the old soul lies
    And never a sound hears she.

From corner to corner he runs about,
  And into the cupboard he peeps;
He rattles the door and bumps on the floor,
  But still the old wife sleeps.

Jangle and bang go the pots and pans,
  As he throws them all around;
And the plates and mugs and dishes and jugs,
  He flings them all to the ground.

Madly the ghost tears up and down
  And screams like a storm at sea;
And at last the old wife stirs in her bed—
  And it's "Drat those mice," says she.

Then the first cock crows and morning shows
  And the troublesome ghost's away.
But, oh, what a pickle the poor wife sees
  When she gets up next day.

"Them's tidy big mice," the old wife thinks,
   And off she goes to Hitchin,
And a tidy big cat she fetches back
   To keep the mice from her kitchen.

—*James Reeves*

I'm such a quiet little ghost,
    Demure and inoffensive,
The other spirits say I'm most
    Absurdly apprehensive.

Through all the merry hours of night
    I'm uniformly cheerful;
I love the dark; but in the light,
    I own I'm rather fearful.

Each dawn I cower down in bed,
    In every brightness seeing,
That weird uncanny form of dread—
    An awful Human Being!

Of course I'm told they can't exist,
    That Nature would not let them:
But Willy Spook, the Humanist,
    Declares that he has met them!

He says they do not glide like us,
    But walk in eerie paces;
They're solid, not diaphanous,
    With arms! and legs!! and faces!!!

And some are beggars, some are kings,
    Some have and some are wanting.
They squander time in doing things,
    Instead of simply haunting.

They talk of "art," the horrid crew,
    And things they call "ambitions."
Oh, yes, I know as well as you
    They're only superstitions.

But should the dreadful day arrive
    When, starting up, I see one,
I'm sure 'twill scare me quite alive;
    And then—Oh, then I'll be one!

—*Arthur Guiterman*

Little Ghost
cries.
Little Ghost
begs.
Nary
a good
does it do.
"No TV tonight!"
says Papa Ghost.
"The horror show
is too
scary."

—Lilian Moore

The Great Auk's ghost rose on one leg,
Sighed thrice and three times winkt,
And turned and poached a phantom egg
And muttered, "I'm extinct."

—Ralph Hodgson

Three little ghostesses,
Sitting on postesses,
Eating buttered toastesses,
Greasing their fistesses,
Up to their wristesses,
Oh, what beastesses
To make such feastesses!

—*Author Unknown*

Mr. Macklin takes his knife
And carves the yellow pumpkin face:
Three holes bring eyes and nose to life,
The mouth has thirteen teeth in place.

Then Mr. Macklin just for fun
Transfers the corn-cob pipe from his
Wry mouth to Jack's, and everyone
Dies laughing! O what fun it is

Till Mr. Macklin draws the shade
And lights the candle in Jack's skull.
Then all the inside dark is made
As spooky and as horrorful

As Halloween, and creepy crawl
The shadows on the tool-house floor,
With Jack's face dancing on the wall.
O Mr. Macklin! Where's the door?

—David McCord

The stranger in the pumpkin said:
"It's all dark inside your head.
What a dullard you must be!
Without light how can you see?
Don't you know that heads should shine
From deep inside themselves—like mine?
Well, don't stand there in a pout
With that dark dome sticking out—
It makes me sick to look at it!
Go and get your candle lit!"

—*John Ciardi*

After its lid
Is cut, the slick
Seeds and stuck
Wet strings
Scooped out,
Walls scraped
Dry and white,
Face carved, candle
Fixed and lit,

Light creeps
Into the thick
Rind: giving
That dead orange
Vegetable skull
Warm skin, making
A live head
To hold its
Sharp gold grin.

—*Valerie Worth*

From Ghoulies and Ghosties,
Long-leggety Beasties,
And THINGS
That go BUMP in the night,
Good Lord, deliver us!

—*Author Unknown*

Beware, my child,
of the snaggle-toothed beast.
He sleeps till noon,
then makes his feast
on Hershey bars
and cakes of yeast
and anyone around-o.

So when you see him,
sneeze three times
and say three loud
and senseless rhymes
and give him all your
saved-up dimes,
or else you'll ne'er be found-o.

—Shel Silverstein

With many a scowl
And many a frown,
A troll pushed
Stones and boulders down.

The crashing sound
Made town folks wonder:
Is it a troll
Or is it thunder?

But hill folks know.
When boulders roll,
It's always the trick
Of a terrible troll.

—B. J. Lee

Be wary of the loathsome troll
that slyly lies in wait
to drag you to his dingy hole
and put you on his plate.

His blood is black and boiling hot,
he gurgles ghastly groans.
He'll cook you in his dinner pot,
your skin, your flesh, your bones.

He'll catch your arms and clutch your legs
and grind you to a pulp,
then swallow you like scrambled eggs —
gobble! gobble! gulp!

So watch your steps when next you go
upon a pleasant stroll,
or you might end in the pit below
as supper for the troll.

—Jack Prelutsky

I saw a gnome
As plain as plain
Sitting on top
Of a weathervane.

He was dressed like a crow
In silky black feathers,
And there he sat watching
All kinds of weathers.

He talked like a crow too,
Caw caw caw,
When he told me exactly
What he saw,

Snow to the north of him
Sun to the south,
And he spoke with a beaky
Kind of a mouth.

But he wasn't a crow,
That was plain as plain
'Cause crows never sit
On a weathervane.

What I saw was simply
A usual gnome
Looking things over
On his way home.

—*Harry Behn*

Do ghouls
go out
on a rainy day?

When it
splishes and
sploshes,
do
ghouls
wear
ghoul-oshes?

—*Lilian Moore*

There is a song to be sung at night
When nothing is left of you and the light
When the cats don't bark
And the mice don't moo
And nightmares come and nuzzle you
When there's blackness in the cupboards
And the closet and the hall
And a tipping, tapping, rapping
In the middle of the wall
When the lights have one by one gone out
All over everywhere
And a shadow by the curtains
Bumps a shadow by the chair
Then you hide beneath your pillow
With your eyes shut very tight
And you sing
"There's nothing sweeter than
The middle of the night.

I'm extremely fond of shadows
And I really must confess
That cats and bats don't scare me
Well, they couldn't scare me less
And most of all I like the things
That slide and slip and creep."
It really is surprising
How fast you fall asleep.

—Karla Kuskin

By day the bat is cousin to the mouse.
He likes the attic of an aging house.

His fingers make a hat about his head.
His pulse beat is so slow we think him dead.

He loops in crazy figures half the night
Among the trees that face the corner light.

But when he brushes up against a screen,
We are afraid of what our eyes have seen:

For something is amiss or out of place
When mice with wings can wear a human face.

—*Theodore Roethke*

Its echoes,
Its aching stairs,
Its doors gone stiff
At the hinges,

Remind us of its
Owners, who
Grew old, who
Died, but

Who are still
Here: leaning
In the closet like
That curtain rod,

Sleeping on the cellar
Shelf like this
Empty
Jelly jar.

—Valerie Worth

But please walk softly as you do.
Frogs dwell here and crickets too.

Ain't no ceiling, only blue
Jays dwell here and sunbeams too.

Floors are flowers—take a few.
Ferns grow here and daisies too.

Whoosh, swoosh—too-whit, too-woo,
Bats dwell here and hoot owls too.

Ha-ha-ha, hee-hee, hoo-hoooo,
Gnomes dwell here and goblins too.

And my child, I thought you knew
I dwell here . . . and so do you.

—*Shel Silverstein*

A skeleton once in Khartoum
Asked a spirit up into his room;
    They spent the whole night
    In the eeriest fight
As to which should be frightened of whom.

—*Author Unknown*

Right after our Thanksgiving feast
Our turkey's bones went hobblin'
To Joan the wicked witch's house
To be her turkey goblin.

—*X. J. Kennedy*

I'm the local Skeleton
who walks this
street.
This is my beat.
Beware!
I'm not very hairy
but I scare
everyone I meet.

People quiver
when they see me.
They flee me!
They shiver
if they must walk
alone.

Oops, there's a dog.
I must run.
His tail has a wag.
He wants to play tag.
And how he would like a
BONE!

—*Lilian Moore*

There was a witch
The witch had an itch
The itch was so itchy it
Gave her a twitch.

Another witch
Admired the twitch
So she started twitching
Though she had no itch.

Now both of them twitch
So it's hard to tell which
Witch has the itch and
Which witch has the twitch.

—*Alexander Resnikoff*

The witch! The witch! Don't let her get you!
Or your Aunt wouldn't know you the next time she met you!

—*Eleanor Farjeon*

Said the cat to the owl,
With a terrible howl,
  "What is that?"
"Who-o-o!" cried the owl.
"I don't know, stupid fowl!"
  Wailed the cat.

"Now I think I shall swoon!
There it goes past the moon—
  Watch it fly!"
Cried the owl, "Which—which?"
"Yes, yes!" shrieked the witch,
  "It is I!
    WITCH! WITCH!"

—*Elizabeth Hough Sechrist*

1

On Halloween, what bothers some
About these witches is, how come
In sailing through the air like bats
They never seem to lose their hats?

2

Hitchhiking owls, as we have seen,
Ride nicely on this queer machine.
Black cats have been reported too;
Which isn't possible or true.

3

Another thing: if brooms can fly,
Do witches keep them handy-by
To sweep the kitchen floor with, say?
Or do they have them locked away
For private passage through the sky?

4

All witches ride well forward, aim
Their broomstick handles, make no claim
For anything like a magic jet.
Who knows a witch's air speed yet?

—David McCord

Look out! Look out, boys! Clear the track!
The witches are here! They've all come back!
They hanged them high,—No use! No use!
What cares a witch for the hangman's noose?
They buried them deep, but they wouldn't lie still,
For cats and witches are hard to kill;
They swore they shouldn't and wouldn't die,—
Books said they did, but they lie! they lie!

—Oliver Wendell Holmes

The sky was yellow,
the moon was green,
and the little old Witch
whispered:

"Halloween!"

and, at the word,
from an ivied tower
thirteen black bats
in a black bat shower
came fluttering through
the pea-green gloom
and rested there
on the WITCH's BROOM!

(And a Witch's Broom—
pray don't forget—
is a million times faster
than any JET!)
So they went to the moon,
and they circled about,
then they swept and they swept
till they swept it out;
they swept out the moon
and they made their flight—
THERE AND BACK
in a single night.

—Ivy O. Eastwick

This is the story of timid Tim
who thought that witches went after him
when the night was dark and moon was dim.
   Woo-HOO, woo-HOO, woo-HOO.

This is the tale of how Tim one night
didn't start home until candlelight
when the sky was black and the snow was white.
   Woo-HOO, woo-HOO, woo-HOO.

He walked through the woods like a frightened goat,
his muffler twisted around his throat,
expecting to jump at a witch's note:
   "Woo-HOO, woo-HOO, woo-HOO."

Out of the night came a sheep dog's yowl,
which Tim was sure was a witch's howl,
a terrible witch on a wintry prowl.
   Woo-HOO, woo-HOO, woo-HOO.

Tim, the timid, began to race,
certain he sighted a witch's face
back of each shadowy hiding place.
    Woo-hoo, woo-hoo, woo-hoo.

He ran through the woods on his lonely trek
till horrors! a hand went around his neck,
holding his headlong flight in check.
    Woo-hoo, woo-hoo, woo-hoo.

Around his throat went a witch's hand
that jerked poor Tim to a sudden stand.
His heart was water, his legs were sand!
    Woo-hoo, woo-hoo, woo-hoo.

Nobody knows how long he stood
with that hand on his throat in the silent wood
until he could find some hardihood . . .
    Woo-hoo, woo-hoo, woo-hoo.

Then he looked around like a shaky calf,
thinking of words for his epitaph,
and "Oh, ho, ho!" he began to laugh . . .
    Woo-hoo, woo-hoo, woo-hoo.

For what he saw was a funny sight—
it *wasn't* a witch at his throat by night,
but a pine branch pulling his muffler tight!
    Woo-hoo, woo-hoo, woo-hoo.

The more Tim chuckled, the more he thought
how most of his fears were like mufflers caught
and stretched much tighter than mufflers ought.
    Woo-hoo, woo-hoo, woo-hoo.

And the end of this story of timid Tim
is—nevermore, when the night was dim,
did he fear that witches were after him!
    Woo-hoo, woo-hoo, woo-hoo.

—*Aileen Fisher*

You're in the mood for freaky food?
You feel your taste buds itchin'
For nice fresh poison ivy greens?
Try Wicked Witch's kitchen!

She has corn on the cobweb, cauldron-hot,
She makes the meanest cider,
But her broomstick cakes and milkweed shakes
Aren't fit to feed a spider.

She likes to brew hot toadstool stew—
"Come eat, my sweet!" she'll cackle—
But if you do, you'll turn into
A jack-o'-lantern's jackal.

—X. J. Kennedy

Live lizard, dead lizard
Marinated, fried.
Poached lizard, pickled lizard
Salty lizard hide.

Hot lizard, cold lizard
Lizard over ice.
Baked lizard, boiled lizard
Lizard served with spice.

Sweet lizard, sour lizard
Smoked lizard heart.
Leg of lizard, loin of lizard
Lizard a la carte.

—Sonja Nikolay

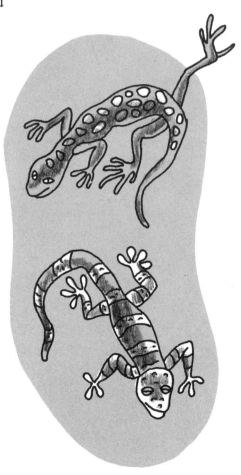

Close your eyes! Feel the
Pale eyeballs of a dead cat—
Two peeled purple grapes.

—*Myra Cohn Livingston*

There was a witch who met an owl.
He flew beside her, wing to jowl.

Owl language always pleased the witch:
Her owl at home sat in his niche
And talked a lot about the bats
He met at night, and how the cats
Were scared of him. That sort of thing.
But here was one owl on the wing,
Who said—I don't mean said "Who, who!"—
Who said, "I've just escaped the zoo.
I'm going home. I haven't flown
Much lately—that is, on my own.
They flew me to the zoo, you know,
Last . . . well, it's several years ago.

"My wings are stiff: I'm tired! *Am* I!
So when I saw you flying by,
I thought 'She's heading north by east.
If I can hitch a ride at least

As far as Pocono, I'll make
It home.' Okay? Is that a rake
Or broom you're flying? Sure! A broom.

"I see it is. Nice model. Room
Enough along the handle for
An owl to perch. Thanks! You can pour
It on! A little shut-eye's what
I need."
   I guess that's what he got.

—*David McCord*

Tonight is the night
When dead leaves fly
Like witches on switches
Across the sky,
When elf and sprite
Flit through the night
On a moony sheen.

Tonight is the night
When leaves make a sound
Like a gnome in his home
Under the ground,
When spooks and trolls
Creep out of holes
Mossy and green.

Tonight is the night
When pumpkins stare
Through sheaves and leaves
Everywhere,
When ghoul and ghost
And goblin host
Dance round their queen.
It's Hallowe'en!

—*Harry Behn*

On Halloween I'll go to town, 13
On Halloween, what bothers some, 64

Right after our Thanksgiving feast, 56

Said the cat to the owl, 63

The Great Auk's ghost rose on one leg, 35
The sky was yellow, 68
The stranger in the pumpkin said, 39
The witch! The witch! Don't let her get you!, 62
There is a song to be sung at night, 50
There was a witch, 61
There was a witch who met an owl, 78
There was an old wife and she lived all alone, 28
This is the story of timid Tim, 70
Three little ghostesses, 36
Tonight is the night, 80
Two ghosts I know once traded heads, 26

We three, 16
Whatever is inside that sheet, 21
When the moon, 24
Witches flying past on broomsticks, 12
With many a scowl, 43

You're in the mood for freaky food?, 74

A coauthor of the *Index to Poetry for Children and Young People*, John E. Brewton has compiled many distinguished anthologies of poetry and verse for children. Born in Brewton, Alabama, Dr. Brewton was graduated from Howard College in Birmingham, Alabama, and received his M.A. and Ph.D. degrees from George Peabody College for Teachers in Nashville, Tennessee. He is now Professor of English, Emeritus, at George Peabody College for Teachers and makes his home in Kingston Springs, Tennessee.

Lorraine Acker Blackburn coauthored with John E. Brewton and George M. Blackburn III the First Supplement to the *Index to Poetry for Children and Young People*, and, with Dr. Brewton, compiled the recently published *They've Discovered a Head in the Box for the Bread and Other Laughable Limericks*. A graduate of George Peabody College for Teachers, she has taught in the metropolitan Nashville school system for the past eight years.

George M. Blackburn III is a coauthor of two volumes of the *Index to Poetry for Children and Young People*, as well as a collection of humorous poetry for children, *My Tang's Tungled and Other Ridiculous Situations*. He has a degree in English from George Peabody College for Teachers and in French from the Sorbonne. Currently he farms, builds log homes, and is engaged in agricultural consulting work.

About the Illustrator

Harriett Barton was born in Picher, Oklahoma, and grew up in nearby Miami. A graduate of the University of Kansas, she presently lives in New York City, where she works as a book designer and illustrates children's books.